THE LITTLE BOOK ABOUT

CHOCOLATE

Published in 2022 by OH!
An Imprint of Welbeck Non-Fiction Limited,
part of Welbeck Publishing Group.
Based in London and Sydney.
www.welbeckpublishing.com

Disclaimer:
This book is intended for general informational purposes only and should not
be relied upon as recommending or promoting any specific practice, diet or
method of treatment. It is not intended to diagnose, advise, treat or prevent
any illness or condition and is not a substitute for advice from a professional
practitioner of the subject matter contained in this book. You should not use the
information in this book as a substitute for medication, nutritional, diet, spiritual
or other treatment that is prescribed by your practitioner. The publisher makes
no representations or warranties with respect to the accuracy, completeness or
currency of the contents of this work, and specifically disclaim, without limitation,
any implied warranties of merchantability or fitness for a particular purpose and
any injury, illness, damage, death, liability or loss incurred, directly or indirectly
from the use or application of any of the contents of this book. Furthermore, the
publisher is not affiliated with and does not sponsor or endorse any uses of or
beliefs about in any way referred in this book.

ISBN 978-1-80069-197-1

Compiled and written by: Catherine Stephenson
Project manager: Russell Porter
Production: Jess Brisley

A CIP catalogue record for this book is available from the British Library

Printed in China

10 9 8 7 6 5 4 3 2 1

Illustrations: The Noun Project

THE LITTLE BOOK ABOUT

CHOCOLATE

PERFECT INDULGENCE

CONTENTS

INTRODUCTION

Over thousands of years, chocolate has made its way from ancient Mesoamerica, through the French Court of Versailles and London's 17th-century chocolate houses, into corner shops and modern five-star restaurants right around the world.

Highly prized and dearly cherished, this edible gold has been an offering to the gods, a currency, a medicine, an aphrodisiac, and a rich draught reserved only for the elite.

Today, chocolate is something a kid can buy with their pocket money, but it is still no less hallowed. For modern-day Western societies, chocolate is childhood, celebration, romance and love. It is special occasions, relationships, emotions. Like wine or bread, it is the food of stories. There is both art and science behind all that creamy, silky perfection.

The easy accessibility of chocolate belies the journey of the cacao bean. It is a long and complex process that starts with the pod of a delicate tree in the tropics, and ends with a production line in Birmingham or Pennsylvania where the finishing touches are made to the ribbon-tied boxes.

Travel the world and chocolate is everywhere. Versatile and steeped in tradition, it takes on a myriad of forms. There are as many different chocolate creations as places and cultures, and while the Sachertorte, the Mars bar and the chocolate digestive may differ in appearance and class, it's chocolate's ability to provide that singular, melt-in-your-mouth moment of pleasure that links them all together.

The constant, over time and geography, is our unswerving fascination with this wonderful food. Wherever you go, there is chocolate, making life that little bit sweeter. If you can't imagine life without it, this book is for you.

CHAPTER
ONE

Food of the Gods

Chocolate has been around for centuries, although the bitter, frothy cacao drinks at the court of King Montezuma were a far cry from the tempting sweet treats of today.

From the Aztecs in Central America, chocolate made its way to the European courts and clergy, but it wasn't until the Industrial Revolution that it became today's sweet pleasure, accessible to all.

In 1753, Swedish scientist **Carl Linnaeus** gave the cacao tree its botanical name, *Theobroma cacao*, Greek for "cacao, food of the gods".

A few hundred years later, millions of chocolate lovers around the world would consider it appropriately named.

The first Mesoamerican culture to domesticate the cacao tree is likely to have been the Olmec, who inhabited the humid lowlands of the Mexican Gulf Coast (c. 1800–300 BCE).

Cacao was sacred for this early civilization. It was used as an offering in religious and marriage ceremonies, in burial rituals and for medicine.

In Mayan mythology, the deity known as the Plumed Serpent gave *kakaw* (cacao) to the Maya after humans were created from maize by the divine grandmother goddess, Xmucane.
A festival was held for the cacao god, Ek Chuah, in April each year.

The cups of chocolate – or *xocolatl*, which is thought to mean "bitter water" – drunk in Mesoamerica as early as 900 CE are a far cry from any you might drink. Cacao beans were toasted and crushed, and then combined with chilli peppers and water to produce a bitter, foamy drink, normally served cold.

Despite the symbolic importance of cacao in the Mayan civilization, it was drunk by ordinary people with their everyday meals.

The Aztecs (13th–16th centuries) loved chocolate. Or rather, their rulers and nobility loved it.

Cacao was highly prized, but unless you were male, wealthy and important, it wasn't readily available.

The Aztec emperor Montezuma may have been the world's first chocoholic.

Legend has it that he drank 50 cups of chocolate from a golden bowl every day.

66

In the province of Nicaragua, a Rabbit is worth ten kernels and for four kernels they give eight apples or loquat of that excellent fruit they call *munonzapot*; and a slave is worth more or less 100 of these kernels, depending on the negotiations between the parties involved.

99

Gonzalo Fernández de Oviedo y Valdés on the value of cacao beans, 1535

Cacao beans were so highly prized by the Aztecs that they used them directly as currency.

Many traders resorted to counterfeiting. People made fakes from clay or materials such as hot ashes, chalk, amaranth dough, wax or avocado pits.

In the Mayan and Aztec civilizations, cacao had important medicinal uses. It was used in brews to treat ailments, such as infections or diarrhoea, and was also used to mask the foul taste of other medicinal ingredients.

Cacao was also known as good for cleaning teeth – although today's dentists might beg to differ.

In the 21st century, a traditional Mexican hot chocolate mixes ground, unsweetened cacao nibs with water, sugar and spices, particularly cinnamon.

At the Wolter chocolate factory on the Hacienda la Luz plantation in Comalcalco, Tabasco, you can see the whole production process, from the field to the table.

It is said that after Spain's Conquest of Mexico, the Aztec emperor, Montezuma, offered the explorer Hernán Cortés and his companions 50 jars of foaming chocolate.

Nobody knows for sure when cacao first reached the Old World, but legend tells it reached Spain after Cortés brought samples back to his king, Charles I, in 1528.

Chocolate is the divine drink which builds up resistance and fights fatigue. A cup of this precious drink permits a man to walk for a whole day without food.

Hernán Cortés

"

[Chocolate] seemed more like a drink for pigs than a drink to be consumed by humans.

"

Italian Girolamo Benzoni in his book *La Historia del Mondo Nuovo*, 1565

When chocolate first arrived in Europe, it was hailed as a powerful aphrodisiac.

Rumours flourished as to how Montezuma drank large quantities of it before cavorting with his numerous wives and concubines.

The bitter and spicy drink that arrived in Europe from the Amazon in the 17th century wasn't everyone's cup of tea.

One observer, José de Acosta, compared the frothy foam chocolate to faeces.

When chocolate was first sweetened with sugar, it went down a treat in Spanish society, especially as it had many purported health benefits. Travellers to the Iberian Peninsula in that period reported, "Chocolate is to the Spanish what tea is to the English."

By the 17th century, chocolate fever had spread across Europe. The boom in demand led to the creation of more cacao plantations and the construction of a trade that relied on a system of forced labour and slavery of Meso-American and African people.

As in Mesoamerica, chocolate was highly regarded as a medicine in Europe. It was also prescribed to improve sexual prowess.

In 1662, the eminent physician Henry Stubbe wrote about the "great use of *Chocolate* in Venery [sexual indulgence], and for supplying the Testicles with a Balsam, or a Sap."

Chocolate was introduced into England around 1652.

One of the first written records appears in Samuel Pepys' diary, the day after the coronation of King Charles II in 1661. Pepys records how he went out for a chocolate in the hope of curing a hangover.

66

Waked in the morning with my head in a sad taking through the last night's drink, which I am very sorry for; so rose and went out with Mr Creed to drink our morning draught, which he did give me in chocolate to settle my stomach.

99

Samuel Pepys' diary entry for 24 April 1661

Charles II – said to have had an equal appetite for sex and chocolate – was perhaps England's first chocoholic.

In 1669, the king spent £229 10s. 8d. on chocolate – more than he spent on tea (only £6), or even on his chief courtesan's allowance (£200).

66

Chocolate symbolizes, as does no other food, luxury, comfort, sensuality, gratification, and love.

99

Karl Petzke, haute cuisine photographer

The chocolate houses of London were the original gentlemen's clubs. Wealthy and respectable men would gather to socialize, do business and talk politics. Some were notorious for heavy drinking and gaming.

London's first chocolate house was opened by a Frenchman in 1657, in Queen's Head Alley near Bishopgate.

Seventeenth-century Londoners were tempted into chocolate houses with the promise of an "excellent West Indian drink".

The hot chocolate of that time was a heady brew with citrus peel, jasmine, vanilla, musk and ambergris.

By 1700, there were as many as 2,000 chocolate houses in London alone.

Some of the City's financial institutions, such as Lloyds of London, are said to have been founded within the wood-panelled walls of chocolate houses.

In the 17th century, chocolate prompted a heated debate within the Catholic Church as to whether or not it was officially a drink and could be consumed on days of fasting.

Eventually Pope Alexander VII settled the matter with a single sentence, *Liquidum non frangit jejunum* ("Liquids do not break the fast"), decreeing that chocolate was indeed a drink.

Such was the craze for chocolate in the 17th century that some wealthy London households had "chocolate kitchens" installed in their homes. They were equipped with chocolate-making devices and often a personal chocolatier.

King Henry VIII's
former home Hampton
Court Palace boasts
a chocolate kitchen
designed by
Sir Christopher Wren,
in 1690.

Three Inventions

Without the Industrial Revolution, chocolate would not have made the transition to the convenient and affordable creamy goodness that we enjoy today. In fact, the shift to mass production of chocolate can be chalked - or chocced - up to three key inventions:

1. *The steam mill*

In 1776, a Frenchman named Doret invented a hydraulic machine to grind cacao seeds into a paste (a job previously done by hand). Not long afterwards, it was succeeded by the steam chocolate grinder, designed by Monsieur Dubuisson.

2. *The hydraulic press*

Invented in 1828 by Dutchman Casparys van Houten, this gadget revolutionized chocolate making. The hydraulic press squeezed the fat from roasted cacao beans to inexpensively and easily make cocoa powder (the basis of all chocolate products).

3. *The alkalization process*

Casparus van Houten's son, Coenraad Van Houten, discovered that if cocoa powder is treated with alkaline salts, it is less bitter, easier to mix with water and has a smoother consistency.

Until 1847, chocolate was only available as a drink.

It was then that the British chocolate company Fry & Sons produced the first solid, rather grainy "eating chocolate" by mixing cocoa butter, sugar and chocolate liquor.

1866 saw the launch
of the first mass-produced
chocolate bar:
Fry's Chocolate Cream.

Amazingly, the original
Fry's Chocolate Cream is
still popular today, and has
been joined by four variants:
peppermint cream, orange
cream, raspberry cream and
strawberry cream.

Swiss chocolatier Daniel Peter of Vevey, Switzerland, invented milk chocolate in 1876.

After eight long years of experimentation and refinement, he perfected the method for dehydrating milk and combining it with chocolate.

By the late 19th and early 20th centuries, family-owned chocolate companies like Cadbury, Mars, Nestlé and Hershey were mass-producing and marketing different types of chocolate to meet a burgeoning demand.

Cocoa Comfort

Early chocolate advertising campaigns
targeted housewives and mothers,
offering them wholesome and hearty
cocoa products for their families:

"Start the day the happy way.
10 seconds to make
DELICIOUS HOT NESTLE'S."

"EPPS'S COCOA.
Grateful and Comforting."

"They're burning energy now.
They'll put it back with
SUPPER-TIME COCOA.
A cup of cocoa is a cup of food.
CADBURY'S BOURNVILLE COCOA."

"More Sustaining Than Meat.
HERSHEY'S Sweet Milk Chocolate."

By 1930, there were nearly
40,000 different kinds of chocolate on
sale in the US.

"

Will looked horrified. 'What kind of monster could possibly hate chocolate?'

"

Cassandra Clare, *Clockwork Angel*, 2010

Grab a Bar!

In the 20th century, affordability and marketing made the chocolate bar everyone's quick and satisfying turn-to treat:

"Go on – Spoil yourself!
Fry's Chocolate Cream"

"Want a Million Dollars Worth of Flavor
for a Dime?... Ask for ALMOND JOY."

"GRAB A BAR"! London.
AT YOUR LOCAL NEWSAGENT

CHAPTER
TWO

It's No Piece of Cake

It all starts with a cacao pod on a faraway tropical tree. Its transformation into a neatly wrapped chocolate bar at the supermarket is no simple feat.

It takes a careful farmer for the delicate tree to flourish; many hands in Africa, Asia or Central America to harvest and pre-process the cacao; a long journey by ship; and a range of specialist factory machinery to package and ready each bar for sale.

Chocolate is the main processed by-product of cacao beans.

They are formed in the pods produced by the cacao "chocolate" tree.

The cacao tree is tropical and can only thrive in hot, rainy climates within 20 degrees north and south of the equator.

It's a very delicate and sensitive plant – it needs shade and also to be sheltered from the wind by other taller trees.

A newly planted cacao seedling is often sheltered by a different tree species.

The cacao tree can actually live up to 200 years.

However, it only produces saleable cacao beans for 25 years.

A cacao tree produces around 30 to 60 pods a year, each of which contains around 40 beans.

It takes as many as 400 cacao beans to make one pound of chocolate.

If you do the maths, you find that each tree only produces around a kilogram (2-3 pounds) of chocolate per year!

At the Cacao Farm

Harvesting

The ripe, orange pods are handpicked
in order to avoid damaging the trees.
They are opened around 10 days later to
extract the wet beans.

Fermentation

The beans are placed in trays covered in
banana leaves and left for 2-7 days.

Drying

The beans are spread out on raised
platforms under the hot sun.
They are turned regularly to ensure
they dry evenly.

Ageing

This takes from 30 days to a year.

Like many food industry producers, individual cocoa farmers are at the mercy of volatile world markets and exploitation by big business.

Today's consumers are increasingly concerned with how their chocolate made the journey from bean to bar, seeking out "ethical chocolate". For example, all Fair Trade certified chocolate has been ethically and sustainably produced.

Although its roots are in Amazonia, almost 70% of the world's cacao comes from four West African countries: the Ivory Coast, Ghana, Nigeria and Cameroon.

The Ivory Coast is the largest single producer with an annual crop of around 1.6 million tonnes.

The Chocolate Industry in Numbers

Over **3 million** tons of cacao beans consumed per year.

Estimated market of **US $138.5 billion** per year.

40-50 million people depend on cacao for their livelihood.

Cacao Beans Compared

Of 11 primary cacao bean varieties, the three most important are:

Criollo, the "Prince of Cocoas".

High-quality, non-bitter, aromatic cocoa.

Origin: Central America, Venezuela, Colombia.

Tricky to produce, expensive and rarely used alone.

Forastero, the versatile one.

Ordinary, everyday cocoa, slightly bitter.

Origin: The Amazon.

Comprises 80-90% of the world's production.

Trinitario, the hybrid.

Fine and rich in fats.

Origin: first produced by introducing Forastero to the local Criollo crop.

Comprises 10-15% of the world's production.

There are thousands of cacao bean hybrids, all specific to the location, climate and soil in which they are grown.

Like the finest wines, choc connoisseurs can discern between different years' harvests.

Legend has it that the Trinitario cacao bean was born in 1727 on the Island of Trinidad, when a hurricane destroyed the local Criollo crops.

The farmers thought all the trees were dead and replanted the plantations with Forastero, but spontaneous hybrids appeared.

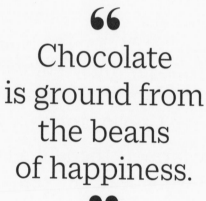

Chocolate is ground from the beans of happiness.

Terri Guillemets

From Bean to Bar

The beans are separated from their pod; fermented to develop their characteristic flavour; and dried, cleaned and roasted.

The cocoa nibs are shelled and ground to make chocolate liquor.

The liquor is cooled and processed into its two components: cocoa solids and cocoa butter.

The sweet chocolate that is so popular today is a combination of cocoa solids, cocoa butter or added vegetable oils, and sugar.

C is for Chocolate:

Cacao beans (n.)
A seed of the cacao tree.

Chocolate liquor (n.)
A bitter liquid or paste produced from
roasted and ground cacao beans.

Chocolatier (n.)
Someone who creates chocolate products
and confections.

Cocoa (n.)
Ground-up cacao with some of the
fat removed.

Cocoa butter (n.)
The natural vegetable fat in a cacao bean.

Chocolate is both an industry and a sensation.

Herman A. Berliner

Conching (n.)
A process in the manufacture of chocolate in which flavour and texture are refined by warming and grinding.

Tempering (n.)
Controlling the temperature of chocolate as it cools and hardens to achieve the best shine, colour, snap and texture.

Rodolphe Lindt invented conching, and he may have done so unintentionally.

The story goes that, when he returned home from the factory one Friday night, he left the mixing machine on. On his return to work on Monday morning, the chocolate in the machine had acquired a silky smooth consistency that he could only have dreamt about.

Chocolate Factory Equipment

1. Sugar Grinding Machine

2. Chocolate Melting Tank

3. Chocolate Conching Machine

4. Chocolate Storage Tank

5. Chocolate Tempering Machine

6. Chocolate Moulding Line

7. Chocolate Packaging Machine

Dark chocolates contain a higher percentage of cacao, whereas ones with lower percentages contain more milk product and sweetener.

The average milk chocolate bar can have as little as 10% of actual cacao bean product, which is the minimum requirement for the FDA to consider a food to be a chocolate product.

White chocolate technically *isn't* chocolate as although it contains cocoa butter, it doesn't contain any cocoa solids.

Fans dispute this, though: a hamburger doesn't contain any ham, and a milkshake is blended, not shaken!

Many argue it makes sense to group white chocolate with the other products made from cacao beans.

Ruby chocolate, also known as "pink chocolate" due to its signature pink colour, debuted in 2017. It was created and patented by Barry Callebaut, which has marketed it as the "fourth type of chocolate" after dark, milk and white.

Sweet and tart, it is described by the manufacturers as having a unique fresh berry taste. Like Willy Wonka, the company is keeping the exact recipe secret...

CHAPTER
THREE

The Eighth Wonder?

If you think chocolate is out of this world, you're not alone.

Chocolate has been cherished since ancient times, and over the centuries it has been ascribed a multitude of properties. It has been linked to religion, to ritual, to our bodies, to medicine, to emotion, to sex.

Why does a simple bean mean so much, to so many people? Let's get to the chocolatey heart of the matter.

The cacao bean has incredibly complex flavours and smells – in fact, it naturally contains around 400 distinct aromas.

To put that in context, roses have 14 and onions just six.

The aromas of different
chocolates are as
varied as melon, citrus,
cherry, berry, raisin,
honey, peach, vanilla,
butterscotch, mint, green
pepper, grass, green olive,
clove, liquorice, leather,
tannin, cedar, tea, coffee
and wine.

66

Look, there's no metaphysics on earth like chocolates.

99

Fernando Pessoa, *The Collected Poems of Alvaro De Campos: 1928–1935*, Vol. 2

Chocolate is known to be a stress-buster and relaxant, as it increases serotonin and endorphin levels in the brain. The endorphin effect is attributed to the sensory properties of chocolate: its unique combination of sweetness, taste and texture. Cocoa butter melts at body temperature, giving you that pleasurable, mouth-watering experience.

Although modern science has found little compelling evidence that the chemical composition of chocolate boosts libido, it has long been valued as an aphrodisiac.

16th-century Aztec ruler Montezuma famously found that his ability to "please the ladies" was enhanced after drinking cocoa.

During the Victorian era, it was feared that the drinking of chocolate, much like reading novels, was a lewd and dangerous activity that could inflame passions and lead to wantonness.

5 Ways to Choc Up Your Love Life

Visit a chocolate spa together.

Surprise your partner with a three-course choc dinner.

Try chocolate body painting.

Snuggle up in bed and watch *Charlie and the Chocolate Factory*.

Whisk your loved one away to a chocolate-themed hotel for the weekend.

Anything that activates the joy centre in the brain makes you happy, and therefore protects you. Oddly enough, that's what they do in Harry Potter: the nurse gives the kids chocolates when they've been near the Dementors!

Jane Siberry

Due to its status as a high-energy food, chocolate has been to war more than once.

In the US Civil War, chocolate was fed to the injured to increase energy. It even served on occasion as payment to troops in lieu of money.

66

I've no ammunition.
What use are
cartridges in battle?
I always carry
chocolate instead.

99

George Bernard Shaw, *Arms and the Man*, 1894

In the Second World War,
Hershey produced a special
chocolate bar as an emergency
energy food for US soldiers.

The bar could remain solid up
to 49C (120F) and was resistent
to poison gas.

However, to stop soldiers eating it except in an emergency, it reportedly tasted only "a little better than a boiled potato".

US troops nicknamed Hershey's chocolate bar "Hitler's secret weapon" because of the havoc it wreaked on their bowels.

After about 20 years of
marriage, I'm finally starting
to scratch the surface
of what women want.
And I think the answer
lies somewhere between
conversation and chocolate.

Mel Gibson

Few natural products have been claimed to successfully treat such a wide range of disorders as chocolate.

Over the centuries, its medical uses have ranged from ailments relating to digestion, anaemia and poor appetite to mental fatigue, poor breast-milk production, tuberculosis, gout, kidney stones and lack of sexual appetite.

Food of my Heart

Cacao beans contain naturally occurring polyphenols, and some studies suggest that they reduce blood pressure and have antioxidant properties.

"

A good night's sleep, or a ten-minute bawl, or a pint of chocolate ice cream, or all three together, is good medicine.

"

Ray Bradbury, *Dandelion Wine*, 1957

Reminiscent of childhood memories, luxury, sweetness and sensuality, chocolate is more than just a food – it is therapy.

Christelle Le Ru

It's a No Brainer

Studies show that consuming dark chocolate with a high percentage of cocoa can stimulate neural activity in areas of the brain associated with pleasure and reward, which in turn decreases stress and improves your mood.

THE EIGHTH WONDER?

Chocolate and love have been associated since ancient times. In a Mayan marriage ritual, the bride and groom each exchanged five cacao beans – along with their vows – to seal the ceremony.

Today, whether it's romantic love, self-love and a treat at the end of the day, or a chocolate birthday cake for a friend, giving chocolate is a sign of affection.

> "
> All you need is
> love. But a little
> chocolate now and
> then doesn't hurt.
> "

Charles M. Schulz

Don't wreck a sublime
chocolate experience
by feeling guilty.
Chocolate isn't like
premarital sex. It will
not make you pregnant.
And it always feels good.

Lora Brody

Like a sponge, chocolate absorbs the flavours of the things around it. Carry it in your bag with some mints and you'll get minty chocolate.

Keep it next to your Roquefort in the fridge and expect a pungent surprise!

CHAPTER
FOUR

Choc-o-bloc Culture

"Say it with chocolate" went one of the popular advertising slogans. And we often do. There are museums about chocolate, chocolate city tours, chocolate factory tours and books about chocolate. It has inspired art, literature and films.

Chocolate can be a gift, a thank you, something for celebration, relaxation, comfort or love, but it's always closely tied to our emotions. What's your chocolate story?

Around 80 million Easter eggs are sold each year in the UK alone!

The calendar is full of excuses to reach out chocolate. Not least of all, at Easter.

Traditionally, dyed and painted chicken eggs were given as gifts at Easter. However, chocolate eggs first made their appearance in France and Germany in the early 19th century, including at the court of Louis XIV in Versailles.

The first chocolate egg was produced in the UK by JS Fry in 1873, and Cadbury was quick to follow suit.

The eggs were made with bitter, dark chocolate, and the now-famous "crocodile skin" finish that you still see on Easter eggs was designed to hide little imperfections or cracks in the chocolate.

'Can I come back and
see you sometime?'

'Long as you bring me some
chocolate,' Gramma said, and
smiled. 'I'm partial to chocolate.'

'Gramma, you're diabetic.'

'I'm old, girl. Gonna die
of something. Might as well
be chocolate.'

Rachel Caine, *The Dead Girls' Dance,* **2007**

103

Chocolate Day

7 July is known as Chocolate Day, the anniversary of chocolate's arrival in Europe, said to be on 7 July 1550.

While the accuracy of the date is disputed, there is a broad consensus that there is plenty of reason to celebrate.

7 November is National Bittersweet Chocolate with Almonds Day.

This strangely specific day celebrates one of the oldest known chocolate recipes - dark, bitter chocolate combined with toasted almonds.

While Valentine's Day was very popular among the Victorians, it was Richard Cadbury who had the brilliant idea of selling his chocolates for the occasion.

He packaged them in beautifully decorated heart-shaped boxes with pictures of rosebuds and cupids.

66

Strength is the capacity to break a chocolate bar into four pieces with your bare hands – and then eat just one of the pieces.

Judith Viorst

66

Forget love ... I'd rather fall in chocolate!

99

Anonymous

Classic Choc Moments on Screen

Jean Harlow, in bed with a giant box of chocolates in *Dinner at Eight*, 1933

Augustus Gloop falling into the chocolate river and getting sucked up a tube in *Willy Wonka and the Chocolate Factory*, 1971

Harry Potter and the leaping chocolate frogs on the Hogwarts Express in *Harry Potter and the Philosopher's Stone*, 2001

Lucy and Ethel trying to wrap chocolates on a swiftly moving conveyor belt in the television series *I Love Lucy*, 1952

"

My momma always said life was like a box of chocolates. You never know what you're gonna get.

"

Tom Hanks in *Forrest Gump*, 1994

In San Francisco, pay a visit to classy Dandelion Chocolate, at 740 Valencia Street.

Take a tour around the small-batch chocolate factory, or drop in at their tasting salon for a choco-licious afternoon tea with profiteroles and chocolate soufflé.

Cover-to-Cover Chocolate
Non-fiction must-reads:

1. *Chocolates and Confections: Formula, Theory, and Technique for the Artisan Confectioner* by Peter P. Greweling (2007) – The Bible of Artisan Confectionery.

2. *The True History of Chocolate* by Sophie D. Coe and Michael D. Coe (2013) – The authors draw upon its botany, archaeology and culinary history.

3. *Cocoa* by Kristy Leissle (2018) – The geopolitical side of the industry.

4. *From Bean To Bar: A Chocolate Lover's Guide to Britain* by Andrew Baker (2019) – A celebration of artisan chocolate-making in Britain.

5. *The Science of Chocolate* by Stephen T. Beckett (2018) – The fascinating science behind the deliciousness.

6. *Chocolate Wars: The 150-Year Rivalry Between the World's Greatest Chocolate Makers* by Deborah Cadbury (2011) – The title says it all!

The greatest tragedies were written by the Greeks and Shakespeare ... neither knew chocolate.

Sandra Boynton

Art and chocolate have always been associated.

The Aztecs created incredible decorative vessels to hold chocolate, and chocolate pots were used in European courts – Pablo Picasso painted one in his Cubist period.

Today, chocolatiers blur the lines between food and art, as they vie to produce the most extravagant creations – almost too beautiful to eat.

"Chocolate Room", the work of pop artist Edward Ruscha, comprised an entire room covered with sheets of paper silk-screened with chocolate.

It appeared at the 1970 Venice Biennale, where it was damaged by ants as well as visitors who scratched anti-war slogans on the walls.

In 2003, the piece was acquired by the Museum of Contemporary Art in Los Angeles.

Jump on one of London's Chocolate Ecstasy Tours – the Mayfair tour is the most popular.

Guides steer you through the whole chocolate-making process, peppering their talk with little-known gems about London's chocolatey history.

5 Choc-themed Flicks

For many, enjoying a film isn't complete without a chocolately treat to unwrap. And then, there are those films that actually feature chocolate – that's double the treat!

1. *Willy Wonka and the Chocolate Factory* (1971) – Based on Roald Dahl's famous tale, the film stars Gene Wilder as eccentric chocolatier Willy Wonka.

2. *Like Water for Chocolate* (1992) – Seductive magical realism, centred around Laura Esquivel's 1992 novel of the same name.

3. *Chocolat* (2005) – Inspired by Joanne Harris's 1999 novel, chocolate symbolizes temptation, freedom and indulgence.

4. *Romantics Anonymous* (2011) – Love is in the air for a pair of chocolatiers.

5. *Merci Pour Le Chocolat* or *"Nightcap"* (2011) – A deadly hot-chocolate nightcap makes for an unsettling thriller.

"

Happiness.
Simple as a glass
of chocolate or
tortuous as
the heart. Bitter.
Sweet. Alive.

"

Joanne Harris, *Chocolat*, 1999

In Mexico, hot chocolate is made with water, not milk. The water is brought to a boil and then the chocolate is spooned into it.

A person in a state of arousal or passion is said to be "like water for chocolate."

If you're in London, stop off
at The River Café on
Thames Wharf for a slice
of Nemesis – chocolate cake
at its richest and gooiest.
It's also available as
a take-away or delivery.

Five Museums
Full of Creamy Goodness

1. The Schokoladenmuseum
Cologne, Germany

Highlights include a tropicarium with cacao trees and a 3-metre- (10-foot-) high chocolate fountain.

2. Choco-Story Chocolate Museum
Bruges, Belgium

Housed in one of the city's oldest medieval buildings.

3. ChocoMuseo,
Cusco, Peru

Try the artisanal chocolate made from organic Peruvian beans.

4. The Chocolate Museum
St Stephen, New Brunswick, Canada

St Stephen is officially Canada's Chocolate Town.

5. Museu de la Xocolata
Barcelona, Spain

Admire the fantastic chocolate sculptures.

Brussels Airport boasts that it is the world's largest chocolate outlet – it sells 1.5 kg (3.3 lb) of chocolate per minute, 2 tonnes per day and 800 tonnes per year.

He showed the words 'chocolate cake' to a group of Americans and recorded their word associations. 'Guilt' was the top response. If that strikes you as unexceptional, consider the response of French eaters to the same prompt: 'celebration'.

Michael Pollan, *In Defense of Food: An Eater's Manifesto*, 2008

Visitors to the Hotel Hershey's decadent Chocolate Spa get to bring their wildest chocolate dreams to life.

How about a chocolate-themed bath or a "chocolate fondue wrap" treatment? Or chill out with a cocoa massage or a chocolate-dipped strawberry immersion.

> **“**
> What you see
> before you, my
> friend, is the
> result of a lifetime
> of chocolate.
> **”**

Katharine Hepburn

66

'Without pain, how could we know joy?' This is an old argument in the field of thinking about suffering and its stupidity and lack of sophistication could be plumbed for centuries but suffice it to say that the existence of broccoli does not, in any way, affect the taste of chocolate.

John Green, *The Fault in Our Stars*, 2012

66

Life is like chocolate:
you should enjoy it
piece for piece and
let it slowly melt on
your tongue.

99

Nina Sandmann

66

I listened wide-eyed, stupid.
Glowing by her voice in the
dim light. If chocolate was
a sound, it would've been
Constantine's voice singing.
If singing was a colour, it
would've been the colour of
that chocolate.

99

Kathryn Stockett, *The Help*, **2009**

'The End is Nigh!'
the man shouted.
'Is there still time for
hot chocolate?'
Riley asked.
The-End-is-Nigh guy
blinked. 'Ah, maybe,
I don't know.'

Jana Oliver, *Forbidden*, 2011

When we don't have the words, chocolate can speak volumes.

Joan Bauer

"

Eat chocolate first, destroy the world later.

"

Rick Riordan, *The Ship of the Dead,* **2017**

CHAPTER
FIVE

The World Loves Choco-lot

Some drink it, some eat it, others bathe in it at the spa: a love of chocolate links people and places, whether it's a craft chocolate bar from a San Francisco café, a lovingly baked chocolate *babka* in Warsaw, or a luxuriant hot chocolate in a Madrid *chocolatería*.

In Mexico, chocolate plays an important part in ancient rituals.

For the *Día de la Muertos* ("Day of the Dead"), when the living must fulfil their obligations to the deceased, chocolate offerings are made in either solid or liquid form, and families visit the cemeteries at night accompanied by a hot chocolate.

The Brazilian Brigadeiro is a bite-sized sweet made from condensed milk, cocoa powder and butter, and coated in chocolate sprinkles.

The sweet got its name back in 1946, when Brigadier Eduardo Gomes ran for government in the first national elections in which women had the vote. His supporters sold the treat to raise funds for his campaign.

The French celebrate April Fool's Day with a chocolate-shaped "April Fish", or *Poisson d'Avril*.

Switzerland attracts chocolate lovers from around the globe, but especially in summer when visitors flock to board the "Belle Époque" carriages of the Chocolate Train.

It does a day trip from Montreux to Gruyères and back, and includes a stop at the Maison Cailler chocolate factory in Broc.

Chocolate *babka* is a sweet, braided bread with layers of dark chocolate, traditionally made in Eastern European Jewish communities, especially Ukraine and Poland.

Babka is a word of Slavic origin, meaning "little grandmother" – it is thought the bread was named for the shape of the original cake, which resembled a grandmother's skirt.

Chocolate ice cream bars are nothing unusual, but very few are like Miša, from the Czech Republic.

When you bite into the hard chocolate outer layer you get a mouthful of frozen quark – a sour-milk-based cheese.

12 million Miša are sold every summer, making it the country's number one ice cream!

If you like your hot chocolate thick, dark and strong, then a Spanish *chocolateria* is the place to be.

Order it with *churros* – the hot chocolate makes a delectable dipping sauce for these crispy, deep-fried dough sticks.

Open all hours, the most famous of Madrid's *chocolaterías* is Chocolatería San Ginés (Pasadizo San Ginés, 5).

It's been serving its signature *chocolate con churros* to Madrileños since 1894.

Tim Tam

The Australian biscuit company Arnott is responsible for the signature Tim Tam: a delightful choc-covered chocolate biscuit with a chocolate cream centre.

How to Tim Tam Slam, Australian-style

1. Grab a coffee, tea or hot chocolate.

2. Bite off each end of a Tim Tam biscuit.

3. Place one bitten end in your mouth and dip the other in your hot drink.

4. Now suck, using the Tim Tam as a straw. As the hot drink comes up, the filling will melt.

5. Eat the Tim Tam before it falls apart!

Champorado, a chocolate rice porridge, is a popular Filipino breakfast dish which can be served either hot or cold. Delicious, satisfying and as easy as pie to make!

Ingredients:

1 litre (5 cups) water
210g (1 cup) sticky or glutinous rice
4 pieces tablea chocolate (or 8 tbsp cocoa powder)
100g (½ cup) sugar
120ml (½ cup) evaporated milk

Method:

1. Bring the water to the boil in a deep saucepan over a medium heat.

2. Add the rice and stir. Lower the heat and stir occasionally, until the rice begins to expand.

3. Add the chocolate and stir regularly, until it has melted. Continue to cook until the rice is translucent and the liquid has reduced to the desired consistency.

4. Add the sugar and continue to cook, stirring regularly, until dissolved.

5. Ladle the champorado into bowls, drizzle with evaporated milk and serve hot.

US chocolatier
Milton S. Hershey confected
the first batch of Hershey's
Kisses in 1907.

The distinctive, conical-shaped
chocolates were allegedly
named for the kissing noise in
production as a nozzle plopped
the kisses onto a cooled
conveyor belt.

Anything is good if it's made of chocolate.

Jo Brand

Milton S. Hershey didn't just build a chocolate factory in his home state of Pennsylvania.

He believed that for a business to be successful, the employees had to be happy, and so he planned and built a whole town – Hershey – with schools, parks, churches, recreational facilities, housing and a trolley system.

Today, the Hersheypark theme park is open to the general public.

The Swiss chocolate industry, renowned for its innovation and high quality, is one of the world's biggest producers, with names such as Cailler, Lindt & Sprüngli and Frey.

Equally, Switzerland is a nation of chocolate eaters, with an impressive average annual consumption per person of 8.8 kg (19.4 lb).

Chocolate Lovers League

(Annual per capita
consumption in kg, in 2017)

1. Switzerland 8.8

2. Austria 8.1

3. Germany 7.9

4. Ireland 7.9

5. UK 7.6

6. Sweden 6.6

7. Estonia 6.5

8. Norway 5.8

9. Poland 5.7

10. Belgium 5.6

Are you a twister or a dunker?

Eaters of the Oreo, America's favourite biscuit, fall into two distinct camps: those who twist the biscuit open and eat the filling first, or those who believe the Oreo is best dipped into a glass of milk.

"

Without chocolate,
we would have to
find something else
to do with the fruit
and nuts.

Anthony T. Hincks

The chocolate digestive is a British classic.

Invented by McVitie's in 1925, travel writer Bill Bryson refers to the biscuit as a "masterpiece".

There's a bit of a
Willy Wonka feel to the
McVitie's factory in Harlesden,
London, which churns out
a massive 13 million choc
digestives a day.

The huge factory is filled with
wafting, delicious smells, and
a kind of chocolate river, or
"enrober", covers the biscuits in
chocolatey goodness.

Ordinary
(but extraordinary) Chocolate
Our all-time favourites:

Toblerone
Those triangular wedges allude
to the Matterhorn

Cadbury Dairy Milk
"A glass and a half..."

Reese's peanut butter cups
A combo made in heaven?

KitKat
"Have a break, have a..."

Guylian
The ultimate Belgian melt-in-your-mouth

Ferrero Rocher
The perfect gold-wrapped gift.

Chocolate (n.)

A delicious cure
for a bad day.

> There are four basic food groups: milk chocolate, dark chocolate, white chocolate and chocolate truffles.

Anonymous

The famous Viennese Sachertorte is a chocolate sponge filled with apricot jam and topped with dark chocolate icing.

The recipe was invented by Franz Sacher in 1832 when his employer, Prince Klemens von Metternich, ordered the kitchen staff to create a new sweet for the evening guests. The chef was ill, so it fell to Sacher, a 16-year-old apprentice, to take charge. The rest is history!

Try your Sachertorte with unsweetened whipped cream and serve it with a cup of coffee or a glass of champagne.

As well as being paired with luxury goods like wine, cheese and decadent fruits, chocolate is a gourmet ingredient in cooking.

Imaginative chefs combine it with countless different flavours, such as chilli, truffle, gouda cheese and aubergine. And let's not forget the now famous pairing of dark chocolate and bacon.

I never met a chocolate I didn't like.

Deanna Troi in *Star Trek*

German artisan chocolate maker Georgia Ramon takes white chocolate as the basis for combinations such as organic kale and mustard or salted Sicilian almonds and broccoli.

Dip it in chocolate, it'll be fine.

Anonymous

CHAPTER
SIX

Chocolate Curiosities

For those intrigued by all things chocolate, the world's favourite treat never ceases to surprise. What makes a cacao leaf special? How big was the world's biggest ever chocolate bar? What does the Lady Gaga Oreo look like?

If you think you've got your chocolate wrapped up, check out these fabulous facts!

Champagne and sparkling wines are too acidic to pair with milk or dark chocolate. A sweet bubbly goes well with white chocolate, whereas red wine and dark chocolate complement each other perfectly.

Match the level of sweetness of the wine with that of the chocolate.

"

You're not feeling well, did you not sleep? Chocolate will make you feel yourself again. A thousand times I have thought: she has no chocolate near her, poor child. What will you do?

"

French aristocrat Marie Rabutin-Chantal De Sévigné in a letter to her ailing daughter, 11 February 1671

In the Oreo charts, the classic Oreo biscuit remains the faithful favourite of most Americans. Of their varieties, the runner-up in 2021 was the Lady Gaga Oreo (pink with a green filling), followed closely by the Golden Oreo.

Cacao tree leaves can move 90°, swivelling to catch sunlight and to protect younger leaves.

Cadbury makes a whopping 500 million Creme Eggs a year. That's a big number, considering that they are only on sale between 1 January and Easter Sunday.

The company tried an all-year-round campaign, but it didn't work, as they stopped being "special".

"

There's something special about Creme Egg season ...
We long for it in those long, eggless days of summer and autumn.

Tony Bilborough, Cadbury

Dear Diamond,
We all know who is really a girl's best friend.

Yours sincerely, Chocolate

Anonymous

In 2013, the Belgian post office issued a limited edition of 5,000 stamps that smelt and tasted just like chocolate.

Produced to celebrate the nation's chocolatiers, the stamps' special paper was imbued with a delightful cocoa aroma while the glue melted on the tip of your tongue, just like chocolate.

Is a chocolate maker the same as a chocolatier? The two lines of work are closely related yet distinct:

Chocolate makers make chocolate from cacao beans.

Chocolatiers craft confections from finished chocolate.

George Cadbury Junior released the first Dairy Milk back in 1905.

The famous slogan "With a glass and a half of fresh milk" had to be dropped in 2010 when EU Trading Standards complained it wasn't metric. It now reads: "The equivalent of 426ml of fresh liquid milk in every 227g of milk chocolate".

However, the iconic purple wrapper still shows the picture of a glass and a half of milk.

66

The 12-step
chocolate programme:
NEVER BE
MORE THAN
12 STEPS AWAY
FROM CHOCOLATE!

Terry Moore

World Champion Chocolate Bar

The Guinness World Record for the largest chocolate bar was taken by the British Thorntons PLC in 2011.

Length: 4 metres (13 ft)
Width: 4 metres (13 ft)
Thickness: 35 cm (1 ft)
Weight: 5792.50 kg (12,770 lbs)

Chocolate comes from cocoa, which is a tree. That makes it a plant.
So chocolate is salad.

Anonymous

In 2001, a Cadbury chocolate bar was sold for $687 at Christie's, London.

At the time of its sale, it was 100 years old – the wrapped and uneaten bar had travelled with Captain Robert Scott on his first *Discovery* expedition to the Antarctic, from 1901 to 1904.

American chef Ruth Wakefield takes credit for the invention of the choc chip cookie, in the 1930s.

One story goes she was trying to make chocolate cookies, but when the chunks of chocolate in the batter didn't melt in the oven, the iconic choc chip version was born.

During the Second World War, care packages containing chocolate chip cookies were sent to some American soldiers.
As word about the sweet treat spread, demand for the cookies skyrocketed.

The French Las Vegas-based pastry chef and influencer Amaury Guichon creates extraordinary chocolate sculptures, worthy of any museum.

His choc masterpieces reflect his love of fantasy, including a *Game of Thrones* dragon, a Demogorgon (the monster from the TV series *Stranger Things*), and even an incredible phoenix rising from the ashes.

Chocolate is the only foodstuff that melts just below body temperature, at

93°F (34°C).

While this provides its delicious melt-on-your-tongue characteristic, it has been a barrier for distribution to warmer climes.

The two "M"s in M&M stand for the names of their creators, Mars and Murrie. Forrest E. Mars Sr was the founder of Mars, while Bruce Murrie was the son of Hershey Chocolate's president, William F. R. Murrie.

While Mars was in England, he saw how Smarties – chocolate buttons covered with a hard, sweet shell – held up in warm temperatures. Back in the US, he approached Murrie with an idea for a new business venture – and the rest is history!

Melts in
your mouth, not in
your hands!

M&Ms tagline

M&Ms were on the frontline in the Second World War and have also been to space in the hands of NASA astronauts, all thanks to their distinctive sugar coating that keeps the chocolate from melting at the usual temperature.

A new, heat-resistant chocolate recipe has been patented by confectionery giant Mars.

Scientists have replaced the traditional cocoa butter with organic sugar in an attempt to stop the slabs turning into gloop.

A 50g (1.7oz) bar of 75% Ecuadorian dark chocolate has roughly the same amount of caffeine as a shot of espresso or a Starbucks cappuccino.

Snickers, that household favourite choc bar with nougat, peanuts and caramel, was named after a horse. The Mars family's beloved racehorse, Snickers, died shortly before the bar was released in 1930.

In the UK and Ireland, the bar was initially sold under the brand name Marathon. In 1990, it became Snickers to align with the rest of the world.

"

It was like having a
box of chocolates shut
in the bedroom drawer.
Until the box was
empty, it occupied the
mind too much.

Graham Greene, *The Heart of the Matter*, 1948